Presented to

_____

From

_____

LULLA·BIBLE

A Musical Treasury for Mother and Baby

STEPHEN ELKINS
Author

ELLIE COLTON
Illustrator

BROADMAN
& HOLMAN
PUBLISHERS

NASHVILLE, TENNESSEE

This book is lovingly dedicated
to my mother,
Phyllis Sue Elkins,
for her love and devotion
to her family.

Table of Contents

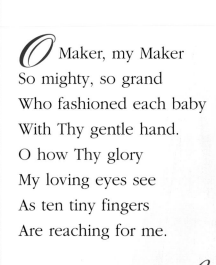

O Maker, my Maker
So mighty, so grand
Who fashioned each baby
With Thy gentle hand.
O how Thy glory
My loving eyes see
As ten tiny fingers
Are reaching for me.

O Maker, My Maker

GENESIS 1:27

Oh Lord I praise you
For this my dear child
Asleep in my arms tonight.
Come tomorrow, I pray
You'll guide us each day
Keep us in Your light.

O Maker, my Maker
Creator and Friend,
For Thine is the glory
And love without end.
O Maker, my Maker
Thy wonders abound.
Let Thy glorious praises
Forever resound.

O Maker, my Maker
Tiny voices prepare
To sing of Thy blessings
And Thy loving care.
The work of Thy hand
We humbly applaud
For my baby was made
In the image of God.

O Lord, bless this child, created in the perfect image of God.

On the Seventh Day God Rested

GENESIS 2:3

On the first day
God made the light,
With His Word it all came
  to be.
Shimmering rays
That dance and play
For all of heaven to see.

On the second day
God made the waters,
And clouds to drift on high.
And light did beam
On glistening streams
That gently trickled by.

On the third day
God made the oceans,
How mighty is our Lord.
To fill the earth
With salty surf
That breaks upon
  the shore.

On the fourth day
God made the starlight,
The sun and moon above.
Who could deny
The evening sky
Was fashioned by His
  love?

On the fifth day
God made the bluebird,
And sparrows all came
  to be.
And fish that swim
Were made by Him
As all beneath the sea.

On the sixth day
God made the animals,
He loved them, every one.
And a man He made

From dust and clay
And then His work was
  done.

On the seventh day
The work was over,
The Lord pronounced
  it good.
And all He'd made
Sang forth His praise
And He rested, as we
  should.

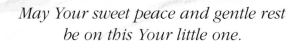

May Your sweet peace and gentle rest
be on this Your little one.

On the Seventh Day God Rested

On the seven-th day the work was o - ver,

the Lord pro-nounced it good;

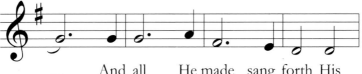

And all He made sang forth His

praise, and He rest - ed as we should.

15

A Walk in the Garden

GENESIS 2:15

Can you imagine
A rose with no thorns?
Bees without stingers,
Bulls without horns?
So perfectly splendid
Eden was made
When God walked with
    Adam
That day.

Come walk,
Come walk in the garden
    with me.
Where the breezes of
    heaven
Blow softly through
    the trees.

Come walk,
Come walk in the garden
    with me.
Together we'll walk with
    our Lord.

Can you imagine
A cat without claws?
Lions that cuddle
Lambs in their paws?
What a wonderful world
Our Father had made
When God walked with
    Adam
That day.

Come walk,

Come walk in the garden
with me.

Where the breezes of
heaven

Blow softly through
the trees.

Come walk,

Come walk in the garden
with me.

Together we'll walk with
our Lord.

Walk with me as I watch over this child
You have entrusted to my care.

A Walk in the Garden

Come walk, come walk in the

gar - den with me, where the

breez - es of heav - en blow

soft - ly through the trees.

Hush-A-Bye Animals

GENESIS 2:19

Hush-a-bye animals,
Hush-a-bye all
Come stand before Adam,
Your name he may call.
Come lions, come tigers
Come elephants too
Hush-a-bye
   animals
Hush-a-bye, do.

I'll call you a "lion"
So loudly you roar.
And you, I'll call "birdie,"
Through skies you will
   soar.

I'll call you "peacock"
With feathers so bright.
And you'll be the "owl"
   To watch over
   the night.

21

Hush-a-bye animals,
Hush-a-bye all.
Come stand before Adam,
Your name he may call.
Come lions, come tigers
Come elephants too.
Hush-a-bye animals
Hush-a-bye, do.

I'll call you "zebra"
Your stripes do abound.
And you'll be my "elephant"
With a trunk hanging down.
And you'll be my
    "duckling"

With a friendly quack,
quack
And I'll call you "turtle"
With the shell on your
    back.

Hush-a-bye animals,
Hush-a-bye all.
Come stand before Adam,
Your name he may call.
Come lions, come tigers
Come elephants too.
Hush-a-bye animals
Hush-a-bye, do.

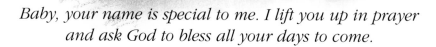

Baby, your name is special to me. I lift you up in prayer
and ask God to bless all your days to come.

Hush-A-Bye Animals

Hush-a-bye an-i-mals, hush-a-bye all;

come stand be-fore A-dam, your

name he may call. Come li-ons, come

ti-gers, come el-e-phants too;

Hush-a-bye an-i-mals, hush-a-bye do.

Noah's Raindrops

GENESIS 7:12

Noah's raindrops
Started falling
Down on the ark,
Down on the ark,
   down on the ark
Noah's raindrops started
   falling
Way down on the ark.
Way down upon the ark.

One little raindrop
Fell on the elephant's trunk
Elephant's trunk,
   elephant's trunk
One little raindrop
Fell on the elephant's trunk
Way down upon the ark.

Two little raindrops
Fell on the kitty-cat's tail
Kitty-cat's tail, kitty-cat's
   tail.
Two little raindrops
Fell on the kitty-cat's tail
Way down upon the ark.

Three little raindrops
Fell on the bunny
   rabbit's ear
Bunny rabbit's ear,
   bunny rabbit's ear.
Three little raindrops
Fell on the bunny
   rabbit's ear
Way down upon the ark.

Four little raindrops
Fell on the puppy
  dog's tail
Puppy dog's tail,
  puppy dog's tail.

Four little raindrops
Fell on the puppy
  dog's tail
Way down upon the ark.

God, just as You sent the rainbow as Your promise,
I promise to raise this child to love You.

Noah's Raindrops

So Many Stars Tonight

GENESIS 15:5

Abraham,
Look to the heavens.
Each star that you see
Is a promise from Me.
Abraham,
Look to the heavens.
Your children will number
Much more than these.

There's one for Isaac.
You'll love him so,
  I know.
There's one for Jacob
To Egypt he'll go.

O look to the heavens
  and believe
Your children will number
  more than these.

Abraham,
Look to the heavens.
Each star that you see
Is a promise from Me.
Abraham,
Look to the heavens.
Your children will
  number
Much more than these.

There's one for David
The shepherd boy.
And one for baby
My dear pride and joy.
O look to the heavens and
believe

Your children will number
more than these.
Just believe
Just believe
Your children will number
more than these.

Thank You for the twinkling stars
that remind us we are
a part of the family of God.

So Many Stars Tonight

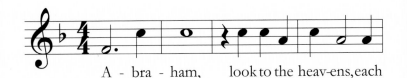

A - bra - ham, look to the heav-ens, each

star that you see is a prom-ise from Me.

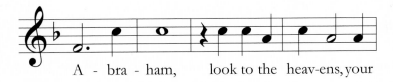

A - bra - ham, look to the heav-ens, your

chil-dren will num - ber much more than these.

Isaac's Lullaby

GENESIS 21:3

Lullaby and goodnight
Go to sleep little Isaac.
Lullaby and goodnight
God is watching o'er us all.

If God wills, thou shalt wake,
When the morning does break.
If God wills, thou shalt wake,
When the morning does break.

Lullaby and goodnight
Go to sleep little baby
Lullaby and goodnight
God is watching o'er us all.

May the blessing of God
Rest upon you, dear child.
May your dreams be so sweet,
Little baby so mild.

*Watch over my slumbering child. Keep this baby safe
all through the day and night.*

Isaac's Lullaby

Lul-la-by and good-night, go to sleep lit-tle Is-aac; Lul-la-by and good-night, God is watch-ing o'er us all.

Jacob's Ladder

GENESIS 28:12

We are climbing
    Jacob's ladder
We are climbing Jacob's
    ladder
We are climbing Jacob's
    ladder
Angel in my arms.

God will watch you
    as you're dreaming
God will watch you
    as you're dreaming
God will watch you
    as you're dreaming
Angel in my arms.

Above the clouds,
  we'll see our Jesus

Above the clouds,
  we'll see our Jesus

Above the clouds,
  we'll see our Jesus

Angel in my arms.

The gates of heaven
  wait before us

The gates of heaven
  wait before us

The gates of heaven
  wait before us

Angel in my arms.

Send Your angels, Lord, to guard this new life.

Jacob's Ladder

We are climb-ing Jac-ob's

lad-der, we are climb-ing Jac-ob's

lad-der, we are climb-ing Jac-ob's

lad-der, an-gel in my arms.

Sleepy-Time Joseph

GENESIS 37:5

Sleepy-time Joseph
Lay down to sleep
His heavy eyes counting
The little white sheep.

Then sleepy-time Joseph
Was slumbering soon
And he dreamed of
  the stars,
The sun, and the moon.
Bow down, bow down,
All shiny stars bow down.
The sun, and the moon,
  and the stars gather
  'round
And they all bow down.

Sleepy-time Joseph
Again knelt to pray.
He thanked his dear
  Father,
Then drifted away.

Then sleepy-time Joseph
A vision he saw,
Bundles of grain
In a field standing tall.
Bow down, bow down,
Bundles of grain bow
   down.
The grain that was bundled
   all gathered around
And they all bow down.

Help me Lord to teach this child to trust in You
as You direct her path.

Sleepy-Time Joseph

Sleep - y - time Jos - eph,— lay down to

sleep, his— heav - y eyes count - ing the

lit - tle white sheep; Then sleep - y - time

Jos - eph was slum - ber - ing soon; And he

dreamed of the stars, the sun, and the moon.

Rock~A~Bye Moses

EXODUS 2:3

Rock-a-bye,
  rock-a-bye,
Rock-a-bye, baby Moses,
  rock-a-bye.
Rock-a-bye, rock-a-bye,
Rock-a-bye, baby Moses,
  rock-a-bye.

Rock-a by faith, the Lord
  is with you
Rock-a by faith, we're safe.
Though waters rise
No need to cry
Rock-a by faith, we're safe,
We're safe!

Rock-a-bye, rock-a-bye,

Rock-a-bye, baby Moses,
   rock-a-bye.

Rock-a-bye, rock-a-bye,

Rock-a-bye, baby Moses,
   rock-a-bye.

Rock-a by faith, He leads
   us home

Rock-a by faith, we're His.

If the winds do blow

This we know

Rock-a by faith, we're His,

We're His!

Rock-a-bye, rock-a-bye,

Rock-a-bye, baby Moses,
   rock-a-bye.

Rock-a-bye, rock-a-bye,

Rock-a-bye, baby Moses,
   rock-a-bye.

Just as You helped Moses' mother to protect her son,
guide me Lord to do the best I can.

Rock-A-Bye Moses

Rock - a - bye,   rock - a - bye, rock-a-

bye,   ba - by   Mo - ses, rock-a - bye;

Rock - a - bye,   rock - a - bye, rock-a-

bye,   ba - by   Mo - ses, rock-a - bye.

Cloud by Day, Fire by Night

EXODUS 13:21

Lord, I can see Your
fire
The desert flame rising
higher.
Clouds they fill the skies,
Lord
Shade our weary eyes,
Lord
Thou art faithful and
evermore shall be.

Oh, Lord with Thy fire
and clouds
Light the way for every
child.

Lead them to Your gates,
Lord
And bless with blessings
great, Lord
For Thou art faithful and
evermore shall be.

Cloud by day, fire by night
Be my joy, my soul's
delight.

Light a path of joy I pray
Melt the bad dreams
    all away.
And when this sleepy day
    has ended
Lord of all, I will ever
    praise You,
I will ever praise You,
I will ever praise You
    Lord of all.

Lord with Thy fire
    and clouds
Light the way for every
    child.
Lead them to Your gates,
    Lord
And bless with blessings
    great, Lord
For Thou art faithful and
    evermore shall be.

Lord, Your love surrounds us day and night.
It is reflected in all of creation.

Cloud by Day,
Fire by Night

Cloud by day, fire by night,

be my joy, my soul's de - light;

Light a path of joy, I pray,

melt the bad dreams all a - way.

The Greatest Blessing

DEUTERONOMY 28:2

I've a blessing of joy
And a blessing of peace.
I've a blessing of gladness
You've poured
  over me.
But surely the
  blessing
Most treasured,
My little child, is you.
Little baby truly it's you.

O when I'm counting
  all my blessings
I've so many, child,
  it's true.
But there's no doubt
  of all my blessings
The greatest blessing
  is you!

I've a blessing of hope
And a blessing of love.
I've a blessing of grace
Sent down from above.
But surely the blessing
Most treasured,
My little child, is you.
Little baby truly it's you.

O when I'm counting all
  my blessings
I've so many, child, it's true.
But there's no doubt of all
  my blessings
The greatest blessing is you!

I've a blessing of family,
Blessings of friends I
  treasure.
The blessings of Jesus
His love never ends
And I am so thankful, Lord.

O when I'm counting all
  my blessings
I've so many, child, it's true.
But there's no doubt of all
  my blessings
The greatest blessing
  is you!

Baby, you are more precious to me than silver or gold.
Thank You God for the blessing of a child.

The Greatest Blessing

O, when I'm count-ing all my bless-ings,

I've so man - y, child, it's true;

But there's no doubt of all my bless-ings,

the great - est bless-ing is you!

Sleepy Little Samson

JUDGES 13:24

When Samson was
  a tiny babe
His mother loved him so.
She knew the Lord had
  touched him
An angel told her so.
With thankful heart,
  she held him close
And kissed his little hands.
To think one day this tiny
  babe
Would be a mighty man!

Samson, Samson
God has called your name.
Samson, Samson
I shall e'er proclaim.
The Lord has been so good
  to me

He's heard my earnest
  prayer.
Rest gently in your mother's
  arms
And know the Lord is there.

I wonder what the future
  holds
For this fair child of God?
I pray for grace and
  blessing

Wherever you may trod.
And may you grow in grace and be
A gentle warrior who,
Might have the strength of Samson
In all you say and do.

Samson, Samson
God has called your name

Samson, Samson
I shall e'er proclaim.
The Lord has been so good to me
He's heard my earnest prayer.
Rest gently in your mother's arms
And know the Lord is there.

God, You have a special plan for this child.
Help him to grow in Your wisdom and strength.

Sleepy Little Samson

When Sam - son was a
ti - ny babe his moth - er loved him
so, she knew the Lord had
touched him, an an-gel told her so.

Hannah's Goodnight Prayer 1 SAMUEL 1:11

Dear Lord, before I
  go to sleep
I lift my voice in praise.
For You, dear Lord, have
heard my prayer
And here Thine answer
  lays.

Dear Lord, I vowed
  before Thy throne
My promise now I keep.
I give this child to You,
  my King
And rest in Thy perfect
  peace.

No greater blessing could there be
No greater blessing known
Than this, a child from heaven sent
But I know he is not my own.

For he is such a special gift
Of grace and love You share.
O thank You, Lord, for this my child
An answer to my prayer.

I hold in my arms the answer to my prayers.
This child of God, Your gift to me.

Hannah's Goodnight Prayer

Dear Lord, be-fore I go to sleep, I

lift my voice in praise; For

You, dear Lord, have heard my prayer, and

here Thine an - swer lays.

63

Samuel Hears God's Voice

1 SAMUEL 3:10

The lamp of God
is burning bright
In the church tonight.
The lamp of God is
burning bright
In the church tonight.

A child named Samuel
is sleeping
In the temple safe
and sound.
A child named Samuel
is sleeping
He awakes, God was
all around.

The doors and windows
opened wide
In the church tonight.
The doors and windows
opened wide
In the church tonight.

The voice of the Lord
was calling
Samuel, listen to His word.

The voice of the Lord was
calling
A voice you have never
heard.

Speak, Your servant is
listening Lord
In the church tonight.
Speak, Your servant is
listening Lord
In the church tonight.

*Help me to teach my child to listen for Your voice
to guide him.*

Samuel Hears God's Voice

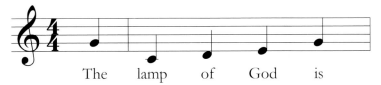

The lamp of God is

burn-ing bright in the church to - night; the

lamp of God is burn - ing bright

in the church to - night.

Now I Lay Me Down to Sleep

PSALM 3:5

*N*ow I lay me down
   to sleep,
I pray the Lord my soul
   to keep.
If I should die before I
   wake,
I pray my soul You'll take.
Keep me safely through
   the night,
Wake me up with morning
   light.
Now I lay me down to
   sleep,
I pray my soul You'll keep.

Now I lay me down
   to sleep,
To dream of mountains tall
   and steep.
Should these mountains
   block my way,
Unto Thee, I'll pray.

Keep me safely through
the night,

Wake me up with morning
light.

Now I lay me down to
sleep,

I pray my soul You'll keep.

Now I lay me down to
sleep,

O Shepherd guard Thy
little sheep.

For in Thy hands our
spirits rest,

And in Thy love we're
blessed.

Keep me safely through
the night,

Wake me up with morning
light.

Now I lay me down to
sleep,

I pray my soul You'll keep.

Bless and keep my child this night and always.

Now I Lay Me Down to Sleep

Now I lay me down to sleep, I
pray the Lord my soul to keep; If
I should die be - fore I wake, I
pray my soul You'll take.

If You Ever Wonder

PSALM 8:3

If you ever wonder,
If you ever ask,
Who made the oceans
And tall fields of grass?
If you ever wonder
Why trees grow so tall
Be certain, baby,
The Lord of heaven
    made it all.

Like the stars in the
    evening sky
He'll be there in the night
    shining for you.
Like the sun that rises high
His light will always shine
    child to guide you.
So rest tonight, be still
Sleep, my child until
The morning light has
    come
And shines on everyone.

If you ever wonder,
If you ever ask,
Who made the flowers
And seasons to pass?
If you ever wonder
Why autumn leaves fall,
Be certain, baby,
The Lord of heaven made
   it all.

Like the waves on a sandy
   shore
He'll wash away the trouble
   in your tender heart.
Like the breeze on a
   mountain tall

He'll breathe His Holy
   Spirit in us all
So rest tonight, be still
Sleep, my child until
The morning light has
   come
And shines on everyone.

If you ever wonder,
If you ever ask,
Who made the flowers
And seasons to pass?
If you ever wonder
Why trees grow so tall
Be certain, baby,
The Lord of heaven made
   it all.

Help me as I teach this precious one all about You, God.

If You Ever Wonder

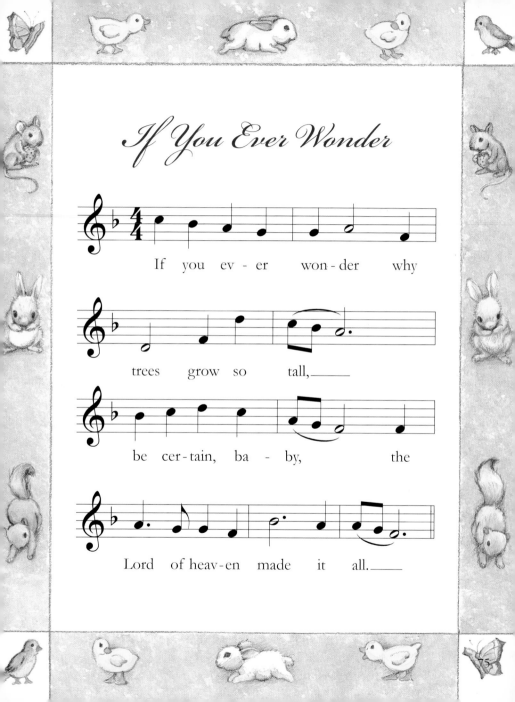

If you ev - er won - der why

trees grow so tall,____

be cer - tain, ba - by, the

Lord of heav-en made it all.____

A Mother's Prayer

PSALM 18:28

Light my candle,
  Holy Spirit
Place Thy holy flame
  in me.
Light my candle,
  Holy Spirit
Shine for all the world
  to see.

Let it shine
Upon my baby
Let it shine
In his heart tonight
Guard each step, O Lord
With Thy flaming sword
And keep the candle
  burning bright.

Light my candle,
  Holy Spirit
Place Thy holy flame
  in me.
Light my candle,
  Holy Spirit
Shine for all the world
  to see.

Let it shine
Upon his way, Lord.
Let it shine
No matter what the cost.
As the years pass away,
This one prayer I pray,
May it lead to Thy precious
cross.

Light my candle, Holy Spirit
Place Thy holy flame in me.
Light my candle, Holy Spirit
Shine for all the world
to see.

Let it shine
Upon my baby
Let it shine
In his heart tonight
Guard each step, O Lord
With Thy flaming sword
And keep the candle
burning bright.

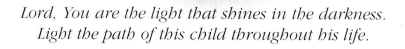

Lord, You are the light that shines in the darkness.
Light the path of this child throughout his life.

A Mother's Prayer

Let it shine___ up-on my ba - by,

let it shine in his heart to - night;

guard each step, O Lord, with Thy flam-ing sword,

and___ keep the can-dle burn-ing bright.

79

The Lord Is My Shepherd

PSALM 23

The Lord is my shepherd
The Lord is my shepherd
The Lord is my shepherd
And I shall not want.

He makes me lie down in
green pastures

He leads me beside still
waters

He restores my soul and
guides me where I go.

The Lord is my shepherd
The Lord is my shepherd
The Lord is my shepherd
And I shall not want.

The Lord is my shepherd
The Lord is my shepherd
The Lord is my shepherd
And I shall not want.

The Lord is my shepherd
The Lord is my shepherd
The Lord is my shepherd
And I shall not want.

*You supply all of our needs. Help me to teach this child
to rely on You.*

The Lord Is My Shepherd

The Lord is my

shep - herd, the Lord is my

shep - herd, the Lord is my

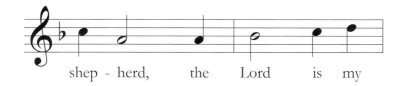

shep - herd and I shall not want.

Cradle Hymn

Lyrics adapted from
a poem by Isaac Watts

PSALM 34:7

Hush, my dear,
lie still and slumber
Holy angels guard thy bed.
Heavenly blessings without
number
Gently falling 'round thy
head.

How much better thou art
attended
Than the Son of God would
be,
When from heaven He
descended
And became a child like
thee.

May you live to know
and fear Him
Trust and love Him all
thy days.
Then go dwell forever
near Him,
See His face and sing
His praise.

How much better thou
art attended
Than the Son of God
would be,
When from heaven He
descended
And became a child like
thee.

I could give thee thousand
   kisses,

Hoping what I most desire,

Not a mother's fondest
   wishes

Can to greater joys aspire.

How much better thou art
   attended

Than the Son of God
   would be,

When from heaven He
   descended

And became a child like
   thee.

*Father, You sent Your Son as a baby because You loved us.
Now I understand the depth of Your love.*

Cradle Hymn

Hush, my dear, lie still and slum - ber,

ho - ly an - gels guard thy bed;

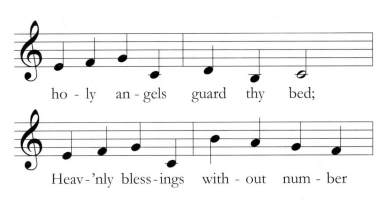

Heav-'nly bless-ings with - out num - ber

gen - tly fall - ing 'round thy head.

The Lord's Lullaby

PSALM 42:8

His song is gentle
His song is peaceful
His song is love
To my baby's heart.
His song is caring,
To tiny baby
His song in heaven
Is the Lord's lullaby.

His song is soothing
His song is mercy
His song is rest
For my baby's soul.
His song the angels
Sing in the evening
His song in heaven
Is the Lord's lullaby.

His song is joyful
His song is patient
His song is comfort
To baby's heart.

His song is precious
Ever endearing
His song in heaven
Is the Lord's lullaby.

*Your songs I'll teach this baby, to hold in her heart
for a lifetime.*

The Lord's Lullaby

His song is gen - tle,

His song is peace - ful,

His song is love to

my ba - by's heart._____

My Little Bed

PSALM 63:6

This little bed is my
  little bed,
The most wonderful place
And let it be said,
When moonbeams dance
Through my sleepy head,
There is no better place
Than my little bed!

My little bed is so perfect,
  you know,
For kneeling and praying
In twilight's glow.
My elbows upon it
My hands folded tight,
I whisper a prayer
By my bed tonight.

This little bed is my little
  bed,
The most wonderful place
And let it be said,
When moonbeams dance
Through my sleepy head,
There is no better place
Than my little bed!

My little bed is so cuddly
and warm,
One fuzzy blanket
With both edges torn.
There's one little pillow
Where I lay my head,
And I am so thankful
For my little bed.

Guard and protect until new morning light,
this child who slumbers tonight

My Little Bed

This lit-tle bed is my lit-tle bed, the most

won-der-ful place, and let it be said, when

moon-beams dance thru my sleep-y head there is

no bet-ter place than my lit-tle bed.

How Innocent

PSALM 116:7

The dark heavy eyelids
  slowly close
On eyes serene and deep.
Upon my breast, my own
  sweet child
Gently falls asleep.

Oh, how fair, how innocent
Like songs the angels gave!
Oh, how fair, how innocent,
That slumbers unafraid.

I kiss his soft and dimpled
cheek
I kiss his rounded chin.
Then lay him on his little
bed
And tuck my baby in.

Oh how fair, how innocent
Like songs the angels gave!
Oh, how fair, how
innocent,
That slumbers unafraid.

*In the sleeping face of my child, God, I see how good
You are to me.*

How Innocent

The dark heav-y eye - lids slow-ly close

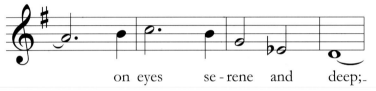

on eyes se - rene and deep;

Up - on my breast, my own sweet

child gent - ly falls a - sleep.

The Lord Never Sleeps

PSALM 121:3

The Lord never sleeps
His strength never fails
He's never frightened
When tempests assail.

Sleep, sleep, sleep
The Lord never sleeps.

The Lord never sleeps
His eyes never close
He guides His children
When troubled winds blow.

Sleep, sleep, sleep
The Lord never sleeps.

The Lord never sleeps
He listens for prayer
Ask Him to comfort
Ask Him to care.

Sleep, sleep, sleep
The Lord never sleeps.

The Lord never sleeps
His love ever flows
From heaven above
To His children below.

Sleep, sleep, sleep
The Lord never sleeps.

The Lord never sleeps
He's always awake
His way you can trust
He makes no mistakes.

Sleep, sleep, sleep
The Lord never sleeps.

The Lord never sleeps
He watches on high
He'll guard you dear baby
While you sleep tonight.

Sleep, sleep, sleep
The Lord never sleeps.

*At the end of the day Lord, I take comfort in the assurance
that You never sleep.*

The Lord Never Sleeps

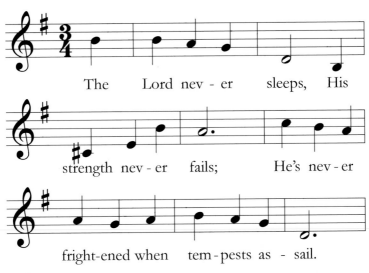

The Lord nev - er sleeps, His

strength nev - er fails; He's nev - er

fright-ened when tem - pests as - sail.

Sleep,——— sleep, sleep,——— the

Lord nev - er sleeps.

Hold Me Jesus

PSALM 139:9-10

Hold me, Jesus
Love and guide me
All through the night.
Hold me, Jesus
Stay beside me
All through the night.

Soft and drowsy
Hours are creeping.
Hill and vale in
  slumber steeping.
My soul Jesus ever
  keeping
All through the night.

Hold me, Jesus
Until morning
All through the night.
Hold me, Jesus
This my yearning
All through the night.

Soft and drowsy
Hours are creeping.
Hill and vale in slumber
    steeping.
My soul Jesus ever keeping
All through the night.

Soft and drowsy
Hours are creeping.
Hill and vale in slumber
    steeping.
My soul Jesus ever
    keeping
All through the night.

I shall not fear the future, for I know You hold this baby
in the palm of Your mighty hand.

Hold Me Jesus

Hold me, Je - sus, love and guide me

all through the night;

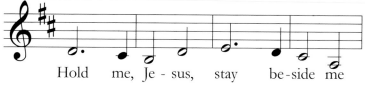

Hold me, Je - sus, stay be - side me

all through the night.

Child Like a Rose

SONG OF SONGS 2:1

Child, like a rose
Your beauty outshines
The bright morning sun
In the summertime.
And your cheeks like her
  petals
Joyfully rise
As you see Mother's eyes.

Child, like a rose
You're beautiful.
Child, like a rose
Gentle and fair.
Child, like a rose
You're beautiful
So beautiful to me.

Child, like a rose
Touched by the dew.
Your hands, like a petal
Are gentle and new
Like a fragrant bouquet.
What rose could compare
To your beautiful face?

Child, like a rose
You're beautiful.
Child, like a rose
Gentle and fair.
Child, like a rose
You're beautiful
So beautiful to me.

Child, like a rose
God fashioned you well.
He's made you so perfect
In every detail.
And your beauty I suppose
Only reflects
The God of the rose.

*God, the delicate beauty of a rose pales in comparison
to the perfect beauty You created in this child.*

Child Like a Rose

Child, like a rose, you're beau-ti-ful,____

Child, like a rose, gen-tle and fair.____

Child, like a rose, you're beau-ti-ful,____ so

beau-ti-ful____ to me.____

The Lion Lays Down with the Lamb

ISAIAH 11:6

Love made the tiger
So gentle and mild.
Love made the lion
A friend of
  a child.
Love was the purpose
Of God's mighty plan.
Yes, love made the lion
Lay down with the lamb.

When God spoke
  the Word
And all came to be,
Love made
  the flower
And love made the bee.
Love made the garden
Of Eden for man,
And love made the lion
Lay down with the lamb.

113

Love made a baby
To laugh and to cry.
Love made a mommy
To sing lullabies.
Love gave us wisdom
That we might understand
Only love makes the lion
Lay down with the lamb.

When God spoke the Word
And all came to be,
Love made the flower
And love made the bee.
Love made the garden
Of Eden for man,
And love made the lion
Lay down with the lamb.

How pure, how innocent the love of this child.
What an awesome reflection of You, God.

The Lion Lays Down with the Lamb

Love made the ti - ger so gen - tle and mild; love made the li - on a friend of a child; Love was the pur - pose of God's might - y plan; Yes, love made the li - on lay down with the lamb.

The Little Shepherd Boy

ISAIAH 40:11

One little sheep is
missing
One little sheep of mine.
1, 2, 3, 4, 5, 6, 7, 8, only 9?
One little sheep is missing
One little sheep I'll find.
1, 2, 3, 4, 5, 6, 7, 8, only 9?

Little shepherd boy
Has a little flock to keep
With his little staff
Watches o'er ten little
sheep.
He counts them very
carefully,
Each and every day.
He sings to them
so merrily
Guides them on their
way.

Wee little shepherd finds
  him
Brings him home again
1, 2, 3, 4, 5, 6, 7, 8, 9, 10!
Wee little shepherd finds
  him
Brings him home again
1, 2, 3, 4, 5, 6, 7, 8, 9, 10!

Little shepherd boy
Has a little flock to keep.
With his little staff
Watches o'er ten little
  sheep.
He counts them very
  carefully,
Each and every day.
He sings to them so
  merrily
Guides them on their way.

O Great Shepherd, gently gather this little lamb
into the safety of Your arms.

The Little Shepherd Boy

Lit-tle Shep-herd Boy has a lit-tle flock to keep,

with his lit - tle staff watch-es o'er ten lit-tle

sheep; He counts them ver-y care-ful-ly,

each and ev-'ry day. He sings to them so

mer-ri-ly, guides them on their way.

Mary, Did You Know Then?

MATTHEW 1:23

Mary, when you held
your child
Tiny baby, meek and mild
Did you know those tiny
hands
Would heal the hearts of
man?

Mary, when your babe was
born
On that chilly Christmas
morn
Did you know those gentle
eyes
Would heal all our hurts
inside?

Mary did you know then
All He'd come to be?
Mary did you know then
He had come to set us
free?
Mary did you know then,
Watching Jesus sleep
beneath the stars,
He would live in each
believer's heart?

Mary, when you
touched His lips
Gently brushed His
fingertips

Did you know His words
   would calm
The mightiest raging
   storm?

Mary did you know then
All He'd come to be?
Mary did you
   know then,

He had come to set us free?
Mary did you know then
Watching Jesus sleep
   beneath the stars,
He would live in you, child?
He would live in me, child?
He would live in all
   believer's hearts?

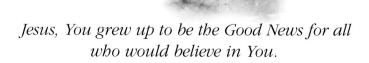

*Jesus, You grew up to be the Good News for all
who would believe in You.*

Mary, Did You Know Then?

Mar - y,——when you held your child,——

ti - ny ba - by, meek and mild;——

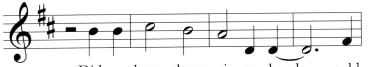

Did you know those ti - ny hands— would

heal the hearts— of men?————

Twinkle, Twinkle Little Star

Twinkle, twinkle
little star
How I wonder what
you are.
Did you shine Your
precious light
On Christ the Lord that
holy night?
Twinkle, twinkle little star
How I wonder what
you are.

Twinkle, twinkle
Bethlehem's star
How I wonder what
you are.
Up above the world
so high
Moving through God's
wondrous sky.
Twinkle, twinkle
Bethlehem's star
How I wonder what
you are.

Twinkle, twinkle Morning
Star

How I wonder who You
are.

Blessed hope of all
mankind

Born to save this heart
of mine.

Twinkle, twinkle Morning
Star

Lord Emmanuel you are!

God, You knew my baby even in the womb.
Help me as I teach her to know all about You.

Twinkle, Twinkle Little Star

Twin - kle,   twin - kle   lit - tle   star,

how   I   won - der   what you   are;

Did you   shine Your   pre - cious   light on

Christ, the   Lord, that   ho - ly   night?

Come Follow Jesus

MATTHEW 4:19

Ten little fingers make
my hands complete
Come follow Jesus, come
follow Jesus.
Ten little toes on the ends
of my feet
Come follow Jesus now.

I've two little eyes that
sparkle and shine
Come follow Jesus, come
follow Jesus.
One little nose I wiggle
sometimes
Come follow Jesus now.

Oh come follow Jesus
Use your fingers and toes
Your eyes and your nose
Come follow Jesus,
Come follow Jesus now.

I've one little mouth that's
smiling so bright
Come follow Jesus, come
follow Jesus.

One little voice to sing
you goodnight
Come follow Jesus now.

Oh come follow Jesus
Let your mouth give Him
glory
Your ears hear the story
Come follow Jesus,
Come follow Jesus now.

Help my child to follow You because You love him so.

Come Follow Jesus

Come   fol - low   Je - sus,   use your

fin-gers and toes,_your eyes and your nose;_

Come   fol - low   Je - sus,

come fol-low Je - sus now.

The Beatitudes

MATTHEW 5:3-9

Blessed are the poor in spirit
Theirs is the Kingdom of Heaven.
Blessed are the poor in spirit
Theirs is the Kingdom of God.

Blessed are the ones who mourn
They will be comforted.
Blessed are the ones who mourn
They will be comforted.

Blessed are the meek in
   spirit,
They will inherit the earth.
Blessed are the meek in
   spirit,
They will inherit the earth.

Blessed are the pure in heart,
They will see God.
Blessed are the pure in heart,
They will see God.

Blessed are the peacemakers,
They will be Sons of God.
Blessed are the peacemakers,
Call them the Sons of God.

Thank You for the blessings a new baby brings,
for they are greater than all the treasures in the world

The Beatitudes

Bless - ed   are   the   poor   in   spir - it,

theirs is the   king-dom of   heav   -   en;

Bless - ed   are   the   poor   in   spir - it,

theirs is the   king-dom of   God._____

This Little Light of Mine

MATTHEW 5:16

This little light of mine,
I'm gonna let it shine.
This little light of mine,
I'm gonna let it shine,
Let it shine, let it shine,
let it shine.

Hide it under a bushel? No!
I'm gonna let it shine.
Hide it under a bushel? No!
I'm gonna let it shine,
Let it shine, let it shine,
let it shine.

When the stars come out
at night,
I'm gonna let it shine.
When the stars come out
at night,
I'm gonna let it shine,
Let it shine, let it shine,
let it shine.

Let it shine 'til Jesus comes,
I'm gonna let it shine.

Let it shine 'til Jesus comes,
I'm gonna let it shine,
Let it shine, let it shine,
let it shine.

This little light of mine,
I'm gonna let it shine.
This little light of mine,
I'm gonna let it shine,
Let it shine, let it shine,
let it shine.

God, shine the light of Your love on this little one.

This Little Light of Mine

This lit-tle light of mine,

I'm gon-na let it shine; This lit-tle light of

mine, I'm gon-na let it shine, let it

shine, let it shine, let it shine.

The Lord's Prayer

MATTHEW 6:9-13

Our Father, which art
in heaven,
Hallowed be Thy name.
Our Father, which art
in heaven,
Hallowed be Thy name.

Thy kingdom come,
Thy will be done
On earth as it is in heaven.
Thy kingdom come,
Thy will be done
On earth as it is in heaven.

Give us this day our daily
bread.
And forgive us our debts
As we forgive our debtors.

Our Father, which art
in heaven,
Hallowed be Thy name.
Our Father, which art
in heaven,
Hallowed be Thy name.

141

And lead us not
Into temptation
But deliver us from evil.
For Thine is the kingdom,
The power and the glory
Forever and ever.

Our Father, which art
    in heaven,
Hallowed be Thy name.
Our Father, which art
    in heaven,
Hallowed be Thy name.

Lord, help me as I teach this child that she can talk
to You anytime, for You are always listening.

The Lord's Prayer

Our Fa-ther, which art   in   heav-en,

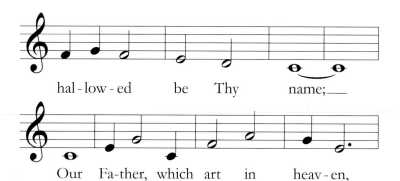

hal-low-ed   be   Thy   name;___

Our   Fa-ther, which art   in   heav-en,

hal-low-ed   be   Thy   name.___

A Sunbeam

MATTHEW 13:43

*L*isten my child,
  to your mother
This verse do I impart,
Know that the love
  of Jesus
Lives within your heart.

A sunbeam, a sunbeam
Jesus wants me for a
  sunbeam.
A sunbeam, a sunbeam
I'll be a sunbeam for Him.

Soon someday child you
  will join Him
And shine for all to see.
Yes, my dear child there's
  a sunbeam
That shines in you
  and me.

A sunbeam, a sunbeam
Jesus wants me for a
  sunbeam.
A sunbeam, a sunbeam
I'll be a sunbeam for Him.

A sunbeam, a sunbeam
Jesus wants me for a
  sunbeam.
A sunbeam, a sunbeam
I'll be a sunbeam for Him.

Lord, bless this child with Your bright inner light
that shines for all to see.

A Sunbeam

A sun - beam, a sun - beam,

Je-sus wants me for a sun - beam; a

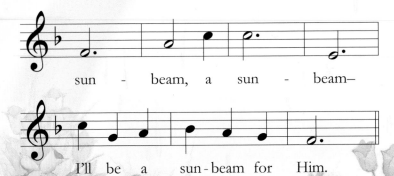

sun - beam, a sun - beam—

I'll be a sun-beam for Him.

Jesus Loves
the Little Children
MATTHEW 19:14

Jesus loves the little children
children
All the children of
the world.
Red and yellow, black
and white,

They are precious in
His sight,
Jesus loves the little
children of the world.

Jesus loves the little
children
All the children of
the world.
When at night they go
to sleep,
Little dreamers He will
keep.
Jesus loves the little
children of the world.

Jesus loves the little
children
All the children of
the world.
Let us thank the Lord
above,
May your dreams be filled
with love.
Jesus loves the little
children of the world.

Jesus loves the little
children
All the children of
the world.
Red and yellow, black
and white,
They are precious in
His sight,
Jesus loves the little
children of the world.

*Thank you God, for the promise that Your love
will never change, never fail, and never leave.*

Jesus Loves the Little Children

Je - sus loves the lit - tle   chil - dren,

all the chil-dren of the   world: red and   yellow,

black and white, they are   pre-cious in His sight;

Je - sus loves the lit-tle chil-dren of the world.

Are You Sleeping, Brother John?

MATTHEW 26:40

Are you sleeping,
Are you sleeping,
Brother John, brother John?
While the Lord is praying,
While the Lord is praying,
Stay awake, stay awake!

Are you sleeping,
Are you sleeping,
Brother James, brother
    James?
While the Lord is praying,
While the Lord is praying,
Stay awake, stay awake!

Are you sleeping,
Are you sleeping,
Brother Peter, brother Peter?
While the Lord is praying,
While the Lord is praying,
Stay awake, stay awake!

*I know that it may not always be easy to do
what You may ask God, so help my child to trust You.*

Are You Sleeping, Brother John?

Are you sleep-ing,　are you sleep-ing

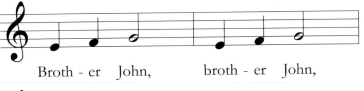

Broth-er John,　broth-er John,

while the Lord is pray-ing,　while the Lord is pray-ing,

stay　a - wake,　stay　a - wake!

155

Sleepy Jesus in a Boat

MARK 4:38

Sleepy Jesus in a boat,
Sleepy Jesus.

The sea was so troubled,
Waves breaking high.
The finger of God
Was swirling the tide.

Twelve brave disciples
That day on the sea,
Up again, down again
Afraid they must be.

156

Sleepy Jesus in a boat,
Sleepy Jesus in a boat,
He's sleeping sound,
    with a storm all around,
Trusting His Father to
    calm the wind down,
Sleep Lord Jesus, sleep
Thy soul Your Father
    will keep.

Peter cried, "Master
The rain's pouring down.
The storm is upon us
I fear we may drown."

Jesus commanded
The wind to obey
And (s-h-h-h!) the wind
    stopped
And they all sailed away.

Sleepy Jesus in a boat,
Sleepy Jesus in a boat,
He's sleeping sound, with
    a storm all around,
Trusting His Father to calm
    the wind down,
Sleep Lord Jesus, sleep
Thy soul Your Father
    will keep.

*Thank You for Your protection God, because I know
I may not always be able to be there.*

Sleepy Jesus in a Boat

Sleep-y Je - sus in a boat;___

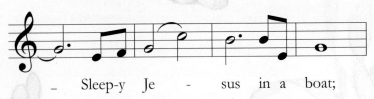

_ Sleep-y Je - sus in a boat;

He's sleep-ing sound with a storm all a-round,

trust-ing His Fa-ther to calm the wind down.

In the Shelter of His Arms

MARK 10:16

I've found a shelter,
Oh so safe and warm.
I've found a shelter safe
in the Master's arms.
I've found a shelter whose
such a peace within,
I'm like a newborn child
The Lord has smiled on me.

In the shelter of His arms
I am safe from all alarm.

I've no fear, no foe can
harm
For great and mighty is
our Savior.
In the shelter of His arms
The things of earth
No longer charm.
So I rest, all is calm
In the shelter of His
arms.

I've found a shelter no
  harm could e'er befall.
I've found a shelter when
  I've no friend at all.
I've found a shelter, a
  haven of delight.
Here I shall ever stay and
  never stray from Him.

In the shelter of His arms
I am safe from all alarm.

I've no fear, no foe can
  harm
For great and mighty is
  our Savior.
In the shelter of His arms
The things of earth
No longer charm.
So I rest, all is calm
In the shelter of His arms.

Baby, of all of God's creation,
you are most the important to Him.

In the Shelter of His Arms

In the shel - ter   of His   arms

I am safe from   all   a - larm;

I've no fear,   no foe can harm,   for

great and might-y   is   our Sav-ior.

Moonlight Prayer

MARK 14:32

Just as the moonlight
shines from above
Touching my baby on
wings of a dove,
God sends His blessing
so gentle and fair
When He hears a
moonlight prayer.

Moonlight prayers
Moonlight prayers
In the ear of the Father
Nothing compares.
Tell Him your troubles
Tell Him your cares
He's waiting for a
moonlight prayer.

Just as the moonlight
illumines the way
And guides little travelers
safe every day,
He holds back the sorrows,
each trouble and care
And answers each
moonlight prayer.

Moonlight prayers
Moonlight prayers
In the ear of the Father
Nothing compares.
Tell Him your troubles
Tell Him your cares
He's waiting for a
moonlight prayer.

*Lay down and sleep my child, for the Father above will
care take of your troubles and fears.*

Moonlight Prayer

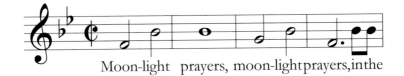

Moon-light prayers, moon-light prayers, in the

ear of the Fa-ther noth-ing com-pares;

Tell Him your trou-bles, tell Him your cares, He's

wait-ing for a moon-light prayer.

God's Angel

LUKE 1:28

As Mary was
praying a long time
ago,
God's angel came,
God's angel came.
As Mary was praying
a long time ago,
The angel Gabriel,
came and said:

"Christ the Lord is
coming soon,
Let the world rejoice
and sing.

Christ the Lord is
coming soon,
Grace and mercy He
will bring."

169

As Joseph was sleeping
a long time ago,

God's angel came, God's
angel came.

As Joseph was sleeping
a long time ago,

The angel Gabriel,
came and said:

"Christ the Lord is
coming soon,

Let the world rejoice
and sing.

Christ the Lord is coming
soon,

Grace and mercy He will
bring."

"Christ the Lord is coming
soon,

Let the world rejoice and
sing.

Christ the Lord is coming
soon,

Grace and mercy He
will bring."

Baby, you are so small yet you represent so much joy.
I pray God's glory will be revealed in your life.

God's Angel

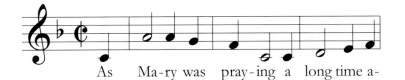

As Ma-ry was pray-ing a long time a-

go,____ God's an-gel came, God's an-gel

came; As Ma-ry was pray-ing a long time a-

go,____ the an-gel Ga-bri-el came

One Precious Moment

LUKE 2:13-14

One precious moment,
One Holy night.
One star was shining
With one precious light.
One night the earth sang
One perfect song,
Messiah's birth, peace
  on earth
Goodwill to all.

In one precious moment
God's love came down
To the hearts of all men.
And there in a manger
The whole world could
  see,
A child's love brought
God's love to me.

One precious moment,
One manger dear.
One child was sleeping
As angels drew near.
One humble stable,
One royal birth.
The angels sang as
  Jesus came
To all the earth.

One precious moment
God's love came down
To the hearts of all men.
And there in a manger
The whole world could
  see,
A child's love brought
  God's love to me.

Christ, because You came as a newborn baby,
my child is an heir of God through You.

One Precious Moment

In one pre - cious mo - ment

God's love came down to the hearts of all

men; And there in a man-ger the whole world could

see a child's love brought God's love to me.

I Will Love You More

LUKE 9:48

Oh, I love you my child
Thou art dearest to me,
Let me hold you evermore.
And when sleepy eyes
  close
And the day finds repose,
Come tomorrow, I will love
  you more.

Oh, I love you my child
Like the bird loves the air,
Like the flower loves
  the rain.
Though my love
  overflows
Still my child, heaven
  knows,
Come tomorrow, I will
  love you more.

Oh, I love you my child
And forever you'll be,
Oh, the dearest to
my soul.
And when morning
doth break
And my child, you awake,
This do know, oh, I will
love you more.

I am comforted because Your love has no end.
Help me as I teach my child to be a reflection of Your love.

I Will Love You More

Oh I love you, my child, thou art

dear - est to me, let me hold you

ev - er - more;___ And when sleep - y eyes

close and the day finds re - pose, come to-

mor - row I will love you more.

Safe in the Shepherd's Arms

LUKE 15:4

Ninety-nine sheep
In the fold, safe and still
Near to the Shepherd's
   heart.
As moonlight fell
On Bethlehem's hill
They were near to the
   Shepherd's heart.

But one sheep
Wandered far away
Away from the
   Shepherd's fold.
And he cried,
   "O Shepherd
I've lost my way.
I'm away from the
   Shepherd's fold."

The Shepherd searched
'Til He found the lamb.
Back in the Shepherd's
arms.
No longer afraid
As He reached out His
hand
He was back in the
Shepherd's arms.

And He carried the
wanderer
Back to the fold.
Safe in the Shepherd's
arms.
Let the love of the
Shepherd
Forever be told.
You're safe in the
Shepherd's arms.

*Bless this little one that he may never lose his
child-like trust of the Master's voice.*

Safe in the Shepherd's Arms

Nine - ty-nine sheep   in the fold, safe and

still   near   to the shep - herd's   heart;___

___ As moon - light fell   on Beth - le-hem's

hill they were near   to the Shep-herd's heart.___

The Light of the World

JOHN 9:5

The sun ever blazes
So brilliantly bright,
  brilliantly bright.
But Jesus shines brighter
He illumines the night,
  illumines the night.

Jesus, the Light of the
  World, the Light of
  the World
The Light of the World.
Oh how He loves each
  boy and girl
Jesus is truly the Light
  of the World.

I've but a candle
A flickering flame,
  a flickering flame.
But Jesus shines through
  me
When I call on His name,
  when I call on His name.

185

Jesus, the Light of the
World, the Light of the
World

The Light of the World.

Oh how He loves each
boy and girl

Jesus is truly the Light
of the World.

The moon is so dazzling

So bright does it shine,
so bright does it shine.

But Jesus shines brighter

No brighter star could
you ever find.

Jesus, the Light of the
World, the Light of the
World

The Light of the World.

Oh how He loves each
boy and girl

Jesus is truly the Light
of the World.

Jesus, Light of the World, shine Your love upon this child,
let him grow to praise Your name.

The Light of the World

Je - sus, the Light of the World, the

Light of the World, the Light of the World;

O how He loves each boy and girl,

Je-sus is tru-ly the Light of the World.

Always in His Hands

JOHN 10:29

Always in His hands,
Always in His hands.
The Lord above is watching
   you tonight,
You are always in His
   hands.
Mighty is the Lord
Upon His Word we stand.
So rest until the morning
   comes, my child
You are always in His
   hands.

Clouds can block the
   sunrise,
Rain can blur the view.
But up above the darkest
   cloud
The sun is shining through.
Nothing is impossible
With our Lord, we can.
So never fear the darkest
   cloud
You are always in His
   hands.

Always in His hands,
Always in His hands.
The Lord above is
  watching you tonight,
You are always in His
  hands.
Mighty is the Lord,
Upon His Word we stand.
So rest until the morning
  comes, my child
You are always in His
  hands.

Troubled winds may blow,
The way becomes unclear.
God will make a way for
  you
So little one, don't you fear.
All things are possible
Our God is so great.
Rest tonight my gentle
  child
The hour is getting late.

*Father, I know that You are in control of all things,
so in faith I give this child back to You.*

Always in His Hands

Al-ways in His   hands,_____

_   al-ways in His   hands;_____

_ The Lord a-bove is watch-ing   you_   to-

night, you are al-ways in His   hands.

He Is My All in All

JOHN 14:6

To the baker, He is the Living Bread.
To the traveler, the Way.
To the builder, He is the Cornerstone
We build upon each day.

To the lawyer, He's the Counselor.
To the teacher, He's the Truth.
To the soldier, He's the Prince of Peace
Though the battle's breaking loose.

To the doctor, the Great Physician.
To the lonely, He's a Friend.
To the preacher, He's the Living Word
A message without end.

But to me He is my all
  in all
He is my all in all.

To astronomers, He is the
  Morning Star.
To the farmer, He's the
  Seed.
To the shepherd, He is the
  Lamb of God
Who meets our every need.

To the weak, He is a
  mighty strength.
To the lost, a Dwelling
  Place.

To the carpenter, He is
  the Door
That opens unto grace.

To the jeweler, He's the
  Living Stone.
To the vine keeper, the
  Vine.
To the banker, He's a
  Treasure great
That everyone must find.

But to me, He is my all
  in all
He is my all in all.

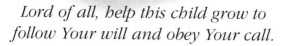

*Lord of all, help this child grow to
follow Your will and obey Your call.*

He Is My All in All

To the bak - er__ He is the Liv-ing

Bread, to the tra - vel -

er, the__ way; To the

build - er,__ He is the Cor-ner - stone we

build up - on each day.

Little Sailor on the Sea

ACTS 27:25

*L*ittle sailor, little sailor
Upon a dreamy sea,
Sailing in a dream boat
To an unknown destiny.
Little sailor, little sailor
Upon a dreamy sea,
Can you see another ship
Sailing next to thee?

It is Jesus walking toward you
On the water coming near.
He is calling out to you child
Have faith and do not fear!

197

Little sailor, little sailor
Upon a dreamy sea,
Sailing in a dream boat
To an unknown destiny.
Little sailor, little sailor
Upon a dreamy sea,
Can you see another ship
Sailing next to thee?

Though the waves spill
  all around you
Do not fear the
  mighty gale.

For yours is but a dream
  boat
With little dreamer sails.

Little sailor, little sailor
Upon a dreamy sea,
Sailing in a dream boat
To an unknown destiny.
Little sailor, little sailor
Upon a dreamy sea,
Can you see another ship
Sailing next to thee?

Though life's storms may come, I pray
that the light of the Son will stay in this child's heart.

Little Sailor on the Sea

Lit - tle sail - or, lit - tle sail - or up-

on a dream-y sea, sail-ing in a

dream boat to an un-known des - ti - ny; Lit-tle

sail - or, lit-tle sail - or up - on a dream-y

sea. Can you see an-oth-er

ship sail-ing next to thee?

No Greater Love

ROMANS 8:39

No greater love has
ever been shown
God takes away every sin
that we've known.
No greater love ever
could be
Than the love that our
Savior has shown to me.

It's greater than the Milky
Way,
It's wider than the widest
sky,
More vast than the
universe,
The love of Jesus Christ.

No greater love has ever
    been shown
God takes away every sin
    that we've known.
No greater love ever
    could be
Than the love that our
    Savior has shown to me.

It's brighter than the
    brightest star,
It's deeper than the
    deepest sea,

It's longer than the longest
    road,
    The love of Christ for me.

No greater love has ever
    been shown
God takes away every sin
    that we've known.
No greater love ever
    could be
Than the love that our
    Savior has shown to me.

God, I know You are watching over Your loved ones.
Thank You for a love that is boundless and free.

No Greater Love

No great-er love___ has ev-er been

shown, God takes a - way ev - 'ry

sin that we've known.___

No great-er love ev - er could

be than the love that our Sav-ior had shown

204

My Lullaby

1 JOHN 4:16

Love
Like an ocean fills my heart
Like a song my soul imparts
Each time I hold you
My soul with rapture thrills.

Love
Like a river flows to you
Like a fountain flows so
   true
Each time I kiss you
My heart just overflows.

You are my life, I live for
   you.
You are the love I hold
   so true.
You are the treasure no
   gold can buy.
You are the only song
   I love to sing,
You are my reason why
My life is so wonderful,
You are my lullaby.

Love
Like a flower in the wind
Like a melody within
My song is for you
I love the things you do.

Love
Like the gentle morning
  rain
Like a singer's sweet refrain
Each time I hold you
My heart is filled
  with song.

You are my life, I live for
  you.
You are the love I hold so
  true.
You are the treasure no
  gold can buy.
You are the only song
  I love to sing,
You are my reason why
My life is so wonderful,
You are my lullaby.

Father, Your promise is one of eternal life.
Thank You for loving us enough to send Your Son.

My Lullaby

You are my life, I live for You,

You are the love I

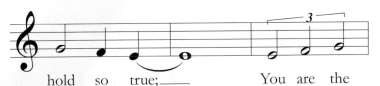

hold so true; You are the

treas - ure no gold can buy.

Jesus Loves Me

1 JOHN 4:19

Jesus loves me
This I know,
For the Bible tells me so.
Little ones to Him
belong,
They are weak but He
is strong.

Yes, Jesus loves me
Yes, Jesus loves me
Yes, Jesus loves me
The Bible tells me so.

Jesus loves me
He who died,
Heaven's gate to open
wide.
He will wash away
my sin,
Let His little child
come in.

Yes, Jesus loves me
Yes, Jesus loves me
Yes, Jesus loves me
The Bible tells me so.

Jesus, take this
Heart of mine,
Make it pure and wholly
    Thine.

On the cross You died
    for me,
I will try to live for Thee.

Yes, Jesus loves me
Yes, Jesus loves me
Yes, Jesus loves me
The Bible tells me so.

Your Word teaches of Your love for us.
Help me to teach this child to love Your Word.

Jesus Loves Me

Je - sus loves me, this I know,

for the Bi - ble tells me so;

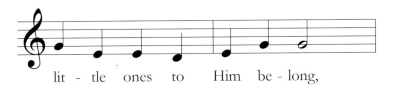

lit - tle ones to Him be - long,

they are weak but He is strong.

One Cloudy Day

REVELATION 1:17

One cloudy day
One cloudy day
The wings of faith will lift
  us high,
To meet our Savior in
  the sky,
One cloudy day
One cloudy day.

One cloudy day
One cloudy day
Christ from whom all
  blessings flow,
Will wake our sleeping
souls below,
One cloudy day
One cloudy day.

One cloudy day
One cloudy day
The Lamb of God from
heaven descends,
And our eternal joy
begins,
One cloudy day
One cloudy day.

The voice of God it
shall be heard,
And all will marvel at
His Word,
One cloudy day
One cloudy day
One cloudy day.

*God, I pray that You will help me to be
a faithful witness to this precious child.*

One Cloudy Day

One cloud-y day,   one cloud-y day   the

wings of faith will   lift   us high   to

meet our Sav - ior   in   the   sky;

One cloud-y   day,   one cloud-y   day.

The Harps of Heaven

REVELATION 14:2

If You come in the morning
What glory that will be,
The saved will meet their Maker
With joyous melody.
If You come in the evening
Thy wonders we'll proclaim
As nightingales sing praises
To Your name.

Hear the sound, hear the sound,
Precious child of God
Hear the sound.
It's the melody of grace coming down,
Let the harps of heaven, harps of heaven
Take you where dreams are found.

If You come in the noonday
And all behold Your face,
The sun could ne'er
  outshine
The wonder of Your grace.
If You come in the
  nighttime
When star and moonlight
  shine,
We'll wake up and
  forever be Thine.

Hear the sound, hear
  the sound,
Precious child of God
Hear the sound.
It's the melody of grace
  coming down,
Let the harps of heaven,
  harps of heaven
Take you where dreams
  are found.

Lord, because You are worthy of all praise,
I'll teach this child to sing songs to You.

The Harps of Heaven

If You come in the morn-ing what

glo - ry that will be, The

saved will meet their Mak - er with

joy - ous mel - o - dy.

Jesus, the Bright and Morning Star

REVELATION 22:5

Jesus, He shines like
diamonds and pearls
On every boy and girl in
the whole wide world.
He shines upon the
meadows,
He shines upon the sea,
He shines in the valley
Wherever you may be.

Jesus is shining on me,
A light for all to see,
And He will ever be
Shining on the hilltops,
On the oceans deep
and wide,
He shines on His children
Who wave His banner
high.

Jesus, He is the Bright
and Morning Star.

Jesus, He shines His light
right where you are.

So as the sun begins to
settle,

Mister Moonlight shines
from afar.

Remember Jesus, He is the
Bright and Morning Star.

Jesus, He shines with
purest true light

In days and darkest nights.

And He shines so bright,

He shines upon my baby

There in the cradle bed.

And may His light guide
you

In all the days ahead.

Jesus is shining on me,

A light for all to see,

And He will ever be shining
on the hilltops,

On the oceans deep and
wide,

He shines on His children

Who wave His banner high.

Child, I pray that you keep Jesus in your heart,
for He is the Light of the World.

Jesus, the Bright and Morning Star

Je-sus,   He is the Bright and Morn-ing Star,

Je - sus, He shines His light right where you   are;

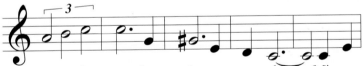

So as the   sun be - gins to   set - tle___ Mis-ter

Moon-light shines from a - far;___Re-mem-ber Je - sus,

He is the   Bright and   Morn - ing   Star.